LITTLE ICE AGE

LITTLE ICE AGE

poems by

MAUREEN SEATON

Maureen Seaton

For David,
With large warm affection!
Maureen
4/30/01

CONTEMPORARY CLASSICS POETRY SERIES
INVISIBLE CITIES PRESS • MONTPELIER, VERMONT

Invisible Cities Press
50 State Street
Montpelier, VT 05602
www.invisiblecitiespress.com

Library of Congress Cataloging-in-Publication Data

Seaton, Maureen, 1947–
Little ice age / Maureen Seaton.
cm. – (Contemporary classics poetry series)
ISBN 0-9679683-7-2 (cloth : alk. paper)
I. Title. II. Series.

PS3569.E218 L5 2001
811'.54—dc21 2001016609

Manufactured in the United States of America

Book design by
Peter Holm
Sterling Hill Productions

FIRST EDITION

for
Denise Duhamel

CONTENTS

The Little Ice Age — ix

I

Romancing Debussy — 3
Vows of Chastity and Indulgence — 4
The Church of Scrabble — 6
Jesus & Puberty — 7
Pluperfect — 8
Nostradamus Predicts the Destruction of New York — 10
When I Wore a Garter Belt — 11
When I Was a Junkie — 12
When I Was a Secretary — 13
When I Was White — 14
When I Was Straight — 15
The Seven Undefined Mathematical Expressions — 16
Lateral Time — 17
Betty — 18

II

Woman Circling Lake — 23
Little Ice Age — 24
Fiddleheads — 25
The Zen of Crime — 27
Priest — 28
Found Liturgy — 30
Astronomy — 31
Torque — 32
Ice — 33
A Flicker of Apocalypse — 34
Endometriosis — 35
Nostradamus Predicts the Destruction of Chicago — 36
Suite for Violence — 37
Near Wild Heaven — 39
Whining Prairie — 40
The Freezing Point of the Universe — 41

III

Miss Molly Rockin' in the House of Blue Light — 45

Acknowledgments — 47

The Little Ice Age
(1645 – 1705)

And snow covered the peoples of North America for sixty years. It covered the ferns and juncos, the snapping turtles and polliwogs. It rusted the bit in the horse's soft mouth and underneath its weight all manner of life slept. The earth, in its curious unnightmared sleep, slept best of all. And when it was time, the snow ceased and the ice passed into memory.

I

Romancing Debussy

Seventeen and sick to death of Bach.
In fact, all those B-boys and their prodigious
Viennese offspring, all those deep
purple pathetiques and crimson gavottes
bored me. I'm a virgin, I said to water lilies, my
own reflection in cologne—I need blue, not
bagatelle or rhythmic blood of birth and war.
Save me, I said in third-year French. *Sauvez*
mon coeur.

———

Daubs of sound divert me from gin fizzes,
that tipsy raft of sneakered fauns
bouncing around gymnasiums with their
pockets bulging. *Wanna kiss?*
They've learned to grope in damp hallways,
facial hair hatching as they speak.
My own fingers meander in sevenths and ninths,
gusts of blue-green breath the boys
call frigid.

———

Once he was a cloud. Once Chagall made him
fly without wings above symphonies,
I saw him at Lincoln Center with the other
nerdy kids who hushed in the dark
as if slain. Oboe, bassoon, first violin!
A hundred little Future Composers of America
poised in their seats with abandon.
Forte, fortissimo, fortississimo: a hundred
contrapuntal climaxes.

———

Before it was over I'd play nothing but his
inventions: "Doctor Gradus ad Parnassum,"
"The Snow Is Dancing . . . ," "Jimbo's Lullaby."
My family propped me up on pillows,
anointed me with oil, thinking I would die
of innocence. My brother imitated crimes
in my honor. My sisters were born.
My parents raised glasses to the genius
in their playroom.

Vows of Chastity and Indulgence

When I was born my mother said she had prayed so long I must be a
miracle.
There was only one way to go with a reputation like that—very bad or
very good.

I chose good and admired the quiet Mary who sat at Jesus' feet and
drank him in,
content to be there with her hair on his arches, oil dripping down his
toes.

Jesus was the only boyfriend I ever wanted. I could be the Virgin Mary
one day, Mary
Magdalen the next—but most of the time I preferred to be his girl, not
his mom.

Thus I chose bad to round myself out and relate to humans, radical
notoriety and
fluent glossolalia at the same time so I could see who was right: Galileo
or the Pope.

Now here I am clumped in a circle of roses red, white, and bittersweet.
All the girls
melting and cohesive, our flames tonguing the walls, banked on universal
principles.

Come all ye faith-filled, goals pre-empted and useless as menstrual blood.
Some think this is the better way, some say we better stop now and get
saved.

Forty-four maidens in a boat and one big mother. Pop!—a leak of sea-
water sprouting
beneath five acres, across the tops of trees. Some women welcome the
same

diversions as men yet need to stay put, we can't help it, we require faith-
fulness.
Now I'm surrounded by Christian memorabilia, some of it pink, some
purple—

Lenten grief and circumstance. A man puts on his special clothes, swal-
lows the bones
of Christ, the eighty-proof claret, lifts the wafer up and brings down
blood and fruit.

There is turbulence in the room, hypervigilance. Never mind the show-off
in the corner,
the wracking cough—proceed to any hallowed place, the sweet marrow
of your own amen.

There is nothing here to mourn, you pretty, the ocean flows over your
right lobe,
everything you expected flows in: succulence, salt, the dark raw deep.

—•—•—•—

The Church of Scrabble

What did she know, after all, nothing! She knew absolutely nothing and no one.
Not true. She knew all things and carried them in her sacred Scrabble bag.

The fragment is a dallier, it has the boundaries of no egg and its starved edges
retreat when you touch them, the right word grabs your ankles and yanks you holy.

This is the river where she carried her prayer to every jetty and cove and one day
she drove to the source in the mountains and drank the river from its solemn mouth.

Belly belly belly belly. The sentence crawls beyond the spit of all that is meant to be.
A brilliant quantum. A terrible faith. The same exact river only older.

Meanwhile, she played word games in various positions and won
according to the moon's grammar, although syntax, rules of grouchy intransitives,

were undesirable. *No one can step into the same river twice!* (Heraclitus)
Watch how geometry yearns at the hands of fools: *awl, labyrinth,*

an old French noun called *swallowwort.* Out like the arms of a tree, down into mud,
subderisorious (mocking, but gently, between friends), *temulency* (inebriation),

a small prank on the double space: *jape.* She played lamely. Once she cheated
with all her vowels spilling to the floor like raw rice or God's blown syllables,

the way they fall upon the people of the earth in a frenzy of triple scores.
She said: Slide back through the cross that used to hang above your bed.

In the middle of wood and bone, you'll find the end and the beginning
of the word you lost, lying on its side like an infant.

Jesus & Puberty

I was the same age as Jesus when he left home and taught in the temple. I sat on the edge of my life—the holy ghost was in my mouth, waters rose and fell around me—and I stepped like an eagle from her nest to begin. I knew everything that had come before, everything that would come after, I guess you could say I was obsessed with the hand gestures little Christ was making in the bible pictures, the way the learned men leaned their heads toward him, the possibilities of all that blood.

My blood descends like a million possible infants. On Halloween we have a party, boy-girl, then down my legs and in my socks, dark jelly, old cherry wine, my childhood slides into earth. Oh God, I say, for the first time meaning damn.

I could grow lighter now but you won't see me in the dark even with these pointy lights pointing blue and cool as raspberry ice. I'm digging deep into loam, forcing myself, a bulb in the thick of earth, everything in me begging to swell and burst. Where will I get the cash to feed my roots, where will my roots go when they've drunk all there possibly is to drink?

Jesus-Jesus-Bo-Besus-Banana-Fana-Fo-Fesus-Fe-Fi-Mo-Mesus. He came to me in his Bo-Besus outfit, soiled but shiny raiment indicative of resurrection, the large sandals made in town by a leather smith. He said my name too softly as always and I was hooked.

Once he took me to the woods behind the brown split-level behind the old stone wall rife with rattlers and placed me on a rock. The rock was cold in summer, cold in winter, it sat below me and drew in my warmth. I was a small iron on its roof and it listened. Jesus flew among trees I named and gave persona to—twin elms, tall virgins. Everywhere fingers of light came down from the Sun, and the child turned the rock warm, the rock blazed bright where the woman-child lay naming trees.

—•—•—•—

Maureen Seaton

Pluperfect

1. Events in life happen.

I want to say I hid beneath school desks in the '50s and thought: *Isn't this ridiculous?* Nuns yelled at us to keep our heads down. Sirens whined. Somewhere in Nevada a test blast melted the hair off a young man's skull, there was nothing left of the pigs and rabbits in uniform, Rita Hayworth's face taped to the bomb like a foreskin. But air raids are peculiar events. They steal something from the *Jane*s of suburban first-grade fictions, tiny believers, pastel peacetime WACs. I kept my head down. No one laughed. Urine leaked out, warm truth.

1. Events in life do not happen, they simply are.

You can always trust the memories of children. Their lives follow into your own, shadow and rebellion, pointed star in your belly drawing blood. Liquor's good: You can fly anywhere and twirl before the Almighty, tremble and spit, a missile crashing into a bedroom window. She was a very sick girl in a bath of ice surrounded by magical interns. The tub teetered like a decision, icy water sloshed, docs sponged her up and down, in and out. In her dream (dream?) they've stolen something, but she can't remember what.

2. Time flows.

They named hurricanes after women: *Alice, Bette, Cornelia.* This made sense: mayhem on a Sunday morning, our mother white-hot still on the Chevrolet's front seat in her feathered hat, her tangerine lips. (Our stinging cheeks, our shoes tied tight.) Or time flows because you can throw a stick in the river and watch it bump toward the sea, down and down, linear as Latin that takes you from logical beginning to predictable end, a whir through time, biting the bones, swallowing the fresh-killed heart of God.

2. No physical experiment has ever detected the flow of time.

And yet the times she tries to die she can't. It's no joke when the kids come bouncing in on her like bombs, pee-soggy and squealing for nourishment. If she lies still they go away, belly down the stairs to dry Cheerios—stick them to the ends of their fingers, pretend they're puppets, bite their heads off. Once, she climbs in the car and drives away, the kids quiet as a losing team in the backseat. Around they go. It's hilarious how the car brings them home. When they open the door to the house, it appears to be waiting.

3. The body is an isolated, self-contained unit.

Fermi took side bets on the possibility that all of New Mexico would blow, atoms bump and pop to infinity, true Laurel and Hardy drama, sanctioned as a father's corporate moves, dragging his family behind him—mama bear and the little bears in their little bear suits. How strange that Fermi stayed in New Mexico for the detonation. My own father was never home, the way the President sits in his oval office, hands folded and immaculate.

3. The body is in dynamic relationship with the universe and all other bodies.

She strains for the sound of her name beneath ice cubes—*B flat,* the key she saves for Sundays and days she calls herself sober. Relatives dig in—salad with baby shrimp, fresh dill weed, cherry tomatoes, a perfect London broil marinated in wine and thyme sprigs, grilled to black and bleeding. Nothing compares to that first buttery bite, everyone says so, it's what she's famous for. They keep her alive for her ability to feed them. Without her they would wander away, dazed with hunger, shimmering with grief.

4. Death is a final, absolute event.

It was because a friend's mother had written the most thorough of notes that Jane decided not to follow suit. They were sitting in the kitchen with the calico cats and the babies begging juice. The small pool in the backyard was shrouded in leaves. Shadows wandered down certain walls. *Here is the note.* Can you imagine? Blue-black ink of a suicide. Silent as a thumb print. Perfect irretrievable light.

4. Since it refers to a body whose matter is not absolute, death is not final.

The first time I saw a dead person I passed out from flowers orbiting the room and giants on my mother's side screaming at each other in a mushroom cloud of smoke. Formaldehyde and carnations. It's said that the blessed take comfort in watching the damned writhe in hell—peering over banisters, angels delight in the agony of souls. Uncle Robby was a stranger to me. I was a little girl in a navy blue pinafore. He was a man so tall they built a special casket. But I knew his feet were curled up in there, elf's feet—that they hurt, like mine in patent leathers. You couldn't fool me. I knew he would wake up mad.

—•—•—•—

from Little Ice Age

Nostradamus Predicts the Destruction of New York

If the bombers in Nostradamus's dream
were to spit toward Manhattan and miss,
just by a hairpin, they'd vaporize me

and my daughters would shimmer greenly
like algae in a beachcomber's footprints.
If the bombers in Nostradamus's dream

blew war on American stockbrokers, mean
as we seem, I'd grieve our misanthropy, twist
like a hairpin as they vaporized me—

You can't judge a nation until it's been
targeted for destruction, blown to bits
by the bombers in Nostradamus's dream,

chemists in trench coats or robes of dreamy
cream. *Oh well,* my daughters say, picking pins
from my hair before bombs vaporize me,

So much for plan A. We prepare for B,
a place to meet when the flames roll in,
when the bombs in Nostradamus's dream
turn on a hairpin and vaporize me.

—•—•—•—

When I Wore a Garter Belt

I was alive before the invention
of panty hose. It was the Golden Age
of Belts—garter, sanitary. Fashion

depended on holding things up, assuaged
cravings you could wear beneath your schoolgirl skirt
and slip, those silky knees, that sudden rage

of nylon hissing down your leg, what hurt
the most: your new *Taupes* fresh from the drugstore,
your fingernail barely brushing, that squirt

of pinkie through *Hanes,* that grief. I was four-
teen, awkward. Notice how my poor nipples
deepened in the night-light dark. Way before

white lace, way before camisoles. The Belt
slipped with gravity until noon when
it lodged tight and cut a groove of welts

around my hips like a skewed and outsized crown
of thorns, studded choke collar gone South. Here's
algebra, I thought, my stockings leaden

with sag at the ankles, crispy skin, where
are the numbers to save me, formula
to ease my body into sweet fifteen? Bare

above the knee, garters etching fabulous
asymmetric circles front and back.
Coarse wool uniform, polyester blouse,

oxfords of substance and sin-ugly. Black
eyeliner circling my eyes like a blur
of wolves. Sexy as the word *attack*.

—•—•—•—

When I Was a Junkie

The junkies are trying to have a decent
conversation. They fool around with
cant for a long time: Stick with the Present,

Lessons in Life Are Free, Choose a Free Gift,
There's No Way Like the American Way.
They know they are excellent athletes, if

sliding down a wall in time to, say,
Stairway to Heaven can be considered
a sport. They're good at what they do, what they

do they might as well do together.
Thus they come to a cusp of desperation
and Run For Their Lives. Says the team of blur:

You think you're alone then perception
shifts, mud slides from your eye to expose
Something—you're this close, nose to nose, fraction

from What The Hell—how should we put this—whose
thrill and quirk is to make night easier,
every move you undertake a rose

on a street of no roses, every desire
a poverty compared to What Is, all
these years you've been looking for it in fire,

in quicksand, there's a pothole and you fall
infinitely into it, your mind
is a crest of Tweetie Birds. After all

the city seems to volley for your time,
back and forth like kisses. Whatever we meant,
say the junkies, we meant to save our lives.

When I Was a Secretary

When I was a secretary hidden
in Food Service like a little mushroom
among the dilettantish aspens

at a school where Kerouac failed to bloom
and the faculty gazed on my stigmata
like royal children, children of *la plume,*

la crème fraîche, I would offer my computer
terza rima and all kinds of unlikely
broilings and inventories. It mattered

less to my word-play that scullions like me
walked invisibly through cafeteria
and washroom, washing hands beside steely

Ph.D.s, than did the gross salaries
of my friends washing dishes. Between rhymes
I infiltrated payroll and squeezed

a spoon's worth of honey from the rich (denied,
of course, if someone had caught me) which I fed
to the poor in sick days and overtime,

six-packs of Pepsi, cold cuts, good red
California burgundy, black caviar.
My words were as reckless as Robin Hood,

my tercets humming with justice and far-
flung anecdotes we laughed over some days.
Most of us lived through poverty. Omar

caught a bullet in his jaw that remains
as we speak. Around us were the children
we served as if their hunger held no blame.

When I Was White

When I was white I came and went, a cycle
of blood and moon and tide, hid nothing
of gun-shape inside me, debated evil

with no one. I said: Bring me something
handsome to eat and they did, that steak butter,
you could spread it on bread. I said: Bring

me taxis. They flew to my side and uttered
Get in and *Where to,* just the thing to carry me.
I said: We are all the same No Matter

What. This was my zaniest folly.
I had blinders on the sides of my head
big as real estate, blue as jelly. We

are all the same Underneath, I said,
and you could count the dusty liberals
nodding in deadly agreement, dead

as the Pope, dead as the Nazis, doornail
dead like the sunnies along Lake Michigan
and the poor bastard steadying his pole

ten feet up the beach. Jesus again,
this time with a sweet brown Chuckie B. face,
and I am beside you in the Bargain

Villa on Clark. I've traveled decades
through dead seas, I've seen my people flap
on their sides as they die of too much shade,

you can count them piling up on the maps
of the world, the unsightly word *equal*
a sticky drool from the Oh of their lips.

When I Was Straight

When I was straight I dreamed of nipples,
my dreams were crowded with cleavage and yin,
I read a book that said if you are fickle

about sex, note your obsession in dreams
then do the opposite in real life. This
made sense, my boyfriend said, although it seemed

oddly like a game of Exquisite Corpse
to me. We'd make love, I'd dream of figs,
that drizzled pink, and sometimes I'd lapse

into madrigals (meaning: of the womb), big
leap from the straightforward sessions in bed
of linearity and menthol. Legs

would cross and uncross in my dreams, heads
fall back with me at the throat. I adored
the winged clavicle, that link between breast-

bone and scapula. Straight as gin, I poured
myself into pretense and fellatio,
you could count on me for bold orgasms, for

trapeze art and graceful aerobics, oh
there is no lover like a panicked lover.
Once I dreamed of abandoning the Old

Boyfriend Theory of Headache and Blunder-
buss. Believe me, I said, this will hurt him
more than me, but the dream laughed! Torture

me, I thought, now that even my id
has turned against me, there is something fragile
here to lose, exquisite truth, and I did.

The Seven Undefined Mathematical Expressions

1. Infinity Divided by Infinity

The moon over Gandhi has age spots and missing teeth. I like the word *ephemeral,* perfect as lake silt, queer as three neutrinos dancing across the Illinois stage. Once I stayed in a dune shack all night, the wind March and freezing. I used all the old man's wood and newspapers dating back to infinity. I was amazing, selfish, hovering like a seabird over skittering pink crabs.

2. Infinity Times Zero

I never told anyone but I can't seem to be together longer than it takes to write one scary poem.

3. Infinity Minus Infinity

I'm sitting on the school bus and Aldo gets on. He smells, but this is his draw, palpable, heady, different from my father at home with his daily aftershave. I hunger for the backseat. High above the rest of the kids, I'd smoke if I knew how. And the girl named Monica (I can say her name now, she'll never read this): I watch her head appear in the stairwell. My breath stopping betrays me and all the angels and saints.

4. Zero Divided by Zero

The same flower repeats itself.

5. Zero to the Zero Power

Cream the butter and both sugars. Add eggs and vanilla; mix together with flour, oatmeal, salt, baking powder, and soda. Add chocolate chips, Hershey Bar and nuts. Roll into balls and place two inches apart on a cookie sheet. Bake for 10 minutes at 375°. Makes 112 cookies.

6. Infinity to the Zero Power

Your mother brought bums into her kitchen and fed them slowly so they wouldn't throw up.

7. One to the Infinite Power

Drumming inside the words, far spaces of quarter past the ninth hole, the justice of each little zen. Keep on until something you say frightens you, but not to the point of murder. Oh, to the point of murder, go on, if you let yourself, there's no reason why you can't live in wind, the strong old oak. It's time to start. Butcher. Silo. Tender conch meat. How we sat and ate seafood with clarified butter and bibs, Lori in her leather tie, me up to my elbows in love.

Maureen Seaton

Lateral Time

I'd never held the ashes of a dead man but I'd always wanted to know a famous artist, so I reached out my left hand and she spilled him into my palm. He was flame-white, his flesh dust, he was tiny bones you could play with—they could be doll parts—peaceful in my hand like light. I kept my hand open in case he needed air and I knew it was not the essence of him but nevertheless I whispered: Don't worry, you're safe with me. I whispered: I love your paintings. This happened on the Upper West Side in '89 as the light changed over the Hudson, and that light was in the apartment sliding on floor and walls as we passed a dead man's bones between us, weeping.

Once I spent the winter in Manhattan with a woman whose desires were so unlike mine the air in the kitchen was sweetly skewed. She told me: *Pleasure,* and I bent at the refrigerator choosing the precise onion. I told her: *Juice,* and she stood at the stove removing lemon seeds from basmati. We were perfect as thumbs, we were starved and greedy as shorebirds, dipping down, grabbing our food, devouring it.

Now I've begun to write "NO!" on my body parts, small cross-stitched reminders to throw me back and hook another. Tattoo on my right breast, sticker on my colon, scribble of bright blue between my ovaries, hollowed now of eggs but still handy to balance me out. The day I decide to go I'll erase the words from my body then disintegrate quickly like any dying fool, you'll see me rising from the shore—equal time lateral time—don't hurry into anything but love.

The man who lives in 4D sleeps above me every night in the same rectangle of space, one floor up, beside the door, our double beds appearing to the gods like open-face sandwiches with two chubby figures shifting and rolling in dreams or trooping to the bathroom. Sometimes I watch Tai Chi on cable at 6 A.M. because the man upstairs has jumped so hard from his bed, and sometimes I sleep right through til 9 or 10, his footfalls barely piercing dawn.

Originally "Body Parts" in The New Republic

Betty

We'll see what happens because something will,
the girlfriend's on third, she's all the way
in her red car, she's here, she's here,
she's home, not the girlfriend I wanted, the one
I'd sleep with without liquor.

There are words I've never drowned in:
woundlessness, kite, little pink tongue.
I am a class of jujube children, the height
of muddy spring. In my hand, a girlfriend with so much love
she thinks I'm hers. Personally
I have a new lease today. A new
relationshipless lease—who can tell if I love it,
who cares if I don't?

Forgive the last one on stage her singleness of mind,
the flowing pièce de résistance, a heartbeat
of jackhammers, pulse one-eighty a minute.
Bring me closer to the high blood pressure machine,
every last bit bathing me like intrepid
soldiers on the rise of a fake hill, Georgia, Atlanta,
a battle close to the saving of the South. I swear,
a morning without new criticism is a morning.
I think I'm on the brink.

I think I'm on the brink.

I think I'm on the brink of, say, a new bike.

I dreamed I was deserted and I was, I dreamed it
again and again until everyone I knew waved.
But I also dreamed about a woman named Jim with damage
to the side of her face: always a wink, always listing into tomorrow.
She loved me loosely. The way certain mothers love their second born.
Here are the words I love today: *total, Hackensack, tenderloin.*
All in all a fine day for words, a peak of syllables.

Toujours! The pen scratches into funny bone,
disproportionate and shaky, fragile
as Amtrak scenery that sways between stations.
My life gets small instead of large and it scares me,
this sanguinity, this exotic perplexity.

I want to write something so lovely my skin melts,
biplane into a vein and create all the fine-tuned June of it.
My failure's aerobic, jumping into drought and scream,

the partnership of Ra and Allah, every little voice zinging home.
Betty. Nothing prepared me for this crux and bell,
a woman dredging synapses.
If I let myself down, I'm foolish. On the rug:
Green. Red. All the children laughing.

Once I thought the world was Irish and Italian.
I will marry one, I thought, like me or unlike me.
I will eat foods from America (hot dogs),
foods from Italy (meatballs), and once a year
cabbage and good corned beef.

I/give/a dime.

I/bring/you cloves.

It's all about tendencies to cook crabs in large pots
before which stands my best friend, Earl,
my best baby boy, my only baby boy-girl. I'm
flattered at the reminiscences of colicky babies,
the reports of sideshows dwelling on the roof
like vegetable gardens and Aunt Rose's begonias.
I once taught red. I held it up for the class to love,
far and away the most conspicuous color, a devil
of foreign standards flowing into icebergs that drift
through Michigan, the last solitude of mummies
when the archaeologist opens the tomb and says: _____.

We camped there, my daughters and I, we had cats
to keep the rats away, drums and strings
and gay flags in the windows. Everyone loved us.
Once we drove down the longest hill in town and the brakes gave.
We put our arms up like on a roller coaster and sped down the mountain.
We landed in a field named Rogers Park. We didn't die.

She said, standing in the bathroom door with her coat protecting her:
Picture me trustworthy. And I am as I write this
with a golden ball in my stomach,
with a light around my head,

with some old tenderness humming.

Meanwhile, we are as late as we can be, all the pieds
and all the pipers, frenzied first kiss,
subways a possibility, the first of May pure as soap.
I don't believe in the taxing of sin.
It's better to receive the coast-clear sound.
Let pages fall around the other poets—I'm outta here.
As they say. All at once
I'm crazy with information like tin cans
rattling in a coffin. Bruises on bone.
High finance and sincerity are the reasons we call ourselves
Americans. It's in our blood.
Red, white, Philadelphia.

I keep positioning the verb between me and another,
the way I climbed into bed between parents—
Jersey, too close to the turnpike, pig farms, oil refineries,
three plane crashes in a row, etc.

The dropping ball, the midtown thunder,
the way I'd somehow drive backwards with my hand
playing like a wand. Bring it up inside me,
all those eggs that once stocked my ovaries.
Three hundred and thirty at least, the size of pinpricks,
quarks and leptons traveling the tube at the speed of life.

There is a point where you defect and nothing happens—
no earth moves, no bolts fly, you stay
your natural color, not blue after all, touched
by prophets of venial sin.

Some wept secretly into hands shaped like steeples,
others slept with their eyes open to receive the light.

—•—•—•—

Woman Circling Lake

Oh transcendent, this aqua blue and all these health nuts
running back and forth hold nothing—no sea gnome,
no salt to scour your bones clean—only placidity
and motionlessness, no dark fugues or phosphorescence.
It's your turn to stir the waters. Don't
back away from brittle plains and dry wheat saying
you're too far above us for encumbrances. This
is your place, your time: Chicago, gate of a millennium.
Your fainthearted sallies fall deep into space, closer
to no one who knows you. See, cloudling, how the collie pup
chases the gray squirrel up bare sleeping trees. How
old snow banks the blue-green line of Michigan.
The collie is so happy and powerful. The squirrel
steals from ash to oak as if possessed by abandon,
rising higher into sky than any jubilant unchained creature.
You are the end of winter, sea light. Little star eater,
come back, it's not your turn to die.

Little Ice Age

I'm not sure how dark you can take it or if you could sit through the night when the violence felt more real than the numb the suburb icy plot she'd lived through traffic streaming 55 the precise meaning of the verb *winter.* It began when the blonde-headed landlord accused them of a certain violence and she let her lover carry her back into the house screaming *This is violence* as if she were proud to be carried as if everyone who saw them on the street would know their particular violence meant love. Something warmer than what she'd had a soul she'd never borne you could count the times before the house on 119 you could take it headfirst the escape you could jump to save your life right through the back window your breaking flesh your legs spectacular. There was no choice about her if it was sex it was sex she remembered her shrink said the insane have good sex but she wouldn't stop when the glacier stopped the husband jerking off so he wouldn't have to learn how to touch her. There was no choice about her lover's arms when they pressed her into walls a floor a chair her body she was there her self not flying to the light as if to watch there was color in her flesh her flesh whole a heat of something connected to something big she'd call God but you might laugh under your breath stupid girl you'd say she'd been so scarred she couldn't find her way out couldn't see she'd called it home that's right it was better than pushing through icefall better than nipping death she just didn't know how to say *enough.*

Fiddleheads

The first time I saw hundreds of fiddlehead ferns boiling in an enormous pot I realized
what an odd person I must be to hear tiny cries from the mouths of cooking vegetables.

Similarly, when you hurt me, I curled like a mouse behind my third eye. I realize what an
odd thing it is to believe as I do in my third eye and the mouse behind it that furls like a fern

and whimpers like a fern being boiled on a monster stove beside its brothers and sisters.
Poor mouse. The things that make a person odd are odd themselves. Think of DNA,

the way it resembles the rope Jack climbed to secure his future and that of his aging Mom.
Or the way a sudden wave can drag a child under, that addiction to adrenalin, her

siblings farther away and more powerless than she ever imagined, the pure and ecstatic
irreversibility of undertow. It's odd to come back to life, as they say, she *came back* to life.

I think I'll come back to life now. It's odd to think of something so big we could miss
the elephant we're living on, like this planet Earth, is she alive and we're her brain cells,

each one of us flickering, going out, coming back to life? Even Chicago looks poignant
from the top of the Hancock, organized and sincere. Think if we were photographing

Earth, how dear she would be, how we'd watch her shimmer in the shimmering black soup
of the firmament, how alone she'd look and how we'd long to protect her, the way it feels

to protect a woman at the height of orgasm, the liquid giving, the seawater slide of
coming back to life. When you hurt me, I evolved like a backboned sea creature, translucent

nervous system sparking along in the meanest deep where I was small enough to not care
my passions ran to swimming, gulping, spitting bubbles back into new oceans.

Once when you hurt me I slept at a Red Roof Inn. I double-locked the door and tried to
watch talk shows to keep my mind off sounds like someone suffocating someone

in the next room. I thought I saw blood on the box spring and imagined needles and bulgy
veins, there's something odd, I thought, about someone whose imagination runs this wild.

So often I dream you're here and I wake in the middle of a prayer from my muzzled
childhood. *Jesus Mary and Joseph,* I say, appalled that I'm stuck in 1955 when I need

something profane to see me through. Serrano's submerged cross. Ginger tea.
The idea that we're moving between horizons and the Earth is so wise she sends us

Winter and red-tailed hawks when we least expect them. *I can do this,* I say,
and the planet shifts imperceptibly. From a great distance she appears to be at peace.

—•—•—•—

The Zen of Crime

I advise her to shoplift something minor,
panties, perhaps, wad of silky skin in her hip pocket.

Or stroll away with coral earlobes, hands
full of jellies or pistachios in harmless white shells.

A side-by-side refrigerator, she says,
and I'll drag it off singing—so you better be there

to bail me out. I tell her my friend
stripped naked and climbed the bars of her cell

making chimp sounds to entertain the other women.
She tells me *her* friend ran from police

into a quarry where she ditched her Mustang
and swam beneath the yellow water to Wisconsin.

Now we begin to admit things: I applied at a topless bar.
I spoke to a madam in Chicago. I stole sirloins

from Dominick's. Like Thelma and Louise. I
was Dillinger in a former life. *I* worked

on Wall Street. Seriously, I say,
what can you steal today to make yourself happy?

Raybans, she says, for the eyes of blind Justice.
All the tea in America.

Priest

I keep dreaming about men. Men who used to be rats running from a sea of broiled light up Liverpool hills who transform before they bite me. It doesn't make sense, this switched syntax. I follow the rat/man around like his tail, all I see is his back (hairy, of course) and the back of his rodent ear-framed head. The dream roils. They say that when the writer begins to write about a dream the reader skips ahead to the dialogue. "Don't leave me," I say, following the man/rat through a city overrun with rats-not-yet-men, but he won't turn around and I can't see his face—would I want to?

Sometimes the men are too young to take seriously. Sarah and I sit in her car divulging: Promise me you won't tell anyone I've got this crush on a guy at work? Me too! I say to make her feel better. There's something about big people, even the young ones, that's comforting. I want to be scooped up, towered over. Just for a few seconds on a Saturday night. I'd sit in his lap like a kitten. He'd rock and we'd watch *Taxi,* the one where Jim's portly father dies and leaves him this huge suit with a cassette tape in the breast pocket. Jim spreads the suit on a chair and the chair reclines. He says, I love you, Dad, then plays the tape. I always cry at this episode, everyone does. *You are the sunshine of my life,* sings Stevie Wonder. Scooped, manipulated, rocked like a little girl.

Sarah says we'd drive the five hours to her uncle's house and shoot him in the balls but we don't have a gun and not only that, we've never seen a gun up close. It would take a lot to accomplish justice in this case. We'd have to find a gun store, no, we'd have to save the money, find a gun store, get a permit, find a shooting gallery, learn to shoot so we don't look stupid or hurt ourselves. She says by the time we get there we'd be diffused, we'd probably peter out somewhere around Gary, and how do people sustain a killing? We think about the art of premeditation, rites and angles of revenge, the unlikeliness of two pissed-off women carrying through on an eye for an eye only lower. Just graze the balls, she says. How do you do that? How about a rubber hose, no marks, tie him up, throw him in the trunk, take him to the woods somewhere, where?—and pummel him.

Once my ex-mother-in-law asked the family for an electric drill. This was years before the cordless ones were invented and we gave our children's Grandma a big Black & Decker and snapped her picture in front of a Douglas fir alight with tradition. There she was fondling the drill like one of her grandchildren. Her Kodak smile looked eerie, as if she'd won something supernatural, something longed for since girlhood. She looked armed, I thought, a long way from home.

In the film *Priest*, a young girl incested by her father asks for help. This in itself is surreal. Then her mother orders her father out of the house and tells the daughter she's Sorry—can you imagine? The final scene shows the girl as she holds a crying priest caught making out with his gay lover in a Volkswagen bug—*Dénouement*. In a review of this flick the director says the love scenes were cause for consternation for the actors playing the two gay characters. That every time she yelled *Cut* they'd leap away from each other, laughing.

—•—•—•—

Found Liturgy

She says there's no god, only an eye here and there that sees clearly.
The neighbors are too busy watching TV to burn her as a witch,

but that doesn't stop her flamboyant behavior on Sunday mornings
while they ready for church, their first-borns savage in their gay

apparel, their babies cuddled in altar silk, everyone pressed
and preened and leaning up the hill toward the steeple that waits,

pointing straight up, in the habit of steeples, toward a cloud shaped
like Olive Oyl shouting at Popeye: *Aw, shut up, you bilge rat!*

Sundays are just right for breaking and entering, she thinks,
baying at the church bells which have begun their jubilant clanging

over consecration. This is the way she holds her own in the world
of prefab sanctuaries and compulsory homage to bible-famed deities.

That is, Sundays she rises naked from her reasonably priced apartment
on Oakley not far from Queen of Angels, some of you may know it,

and wings around the steeple like a Chagall, hands out and up, legs
out and back, torso a pretty blue or, in the case of certain days,

covered in warbler feathers, the traditional gold of the bright fast bird
that people living in cities mistake for pet angels, often try to catch

and pin to their lapels for protection. She, nevertheless, has avoided
mascot-status, although once during a particularly laborious

Easter week service when the pastor had everyone standing for
the entire gospel according to Mark, a little girl, who'd been asleep

on the pew behind her parents, happened to open her eyes
just in time to see the yellow bird with the black mask zoom

past the window. The window depicted a scene often depicted
in churches around the world: The woman at the well with Jesus

in disguise asking for water. Curious to discover the destination
of the tiny being flitting through the stained glass picture which fell

in bloody colors on the floor beside her, the little girl practiced her new
art of astral projection and left her body to explore the skies of Chicago.

There is no moral to this story and that, it's said, is the beauty of it.

Astronomy

You could stay in the blast room all day
unmasked against the fragile ruinous dust.

I could eat these unrecognizable pastries,
white dollops and feminine,

all chalk in my mouth, all glass in yours.
We could continue like this, circumspect

and innocent as a cat on the El tracks,
the ladies from Mexico screaming,

the stout men pushing. And nothing
would budge us. We could be that Irish,

our eyes perceiving Venus miss the moon,
the space between us a clamor of light.

But science adores chance. We could be
walking paranoid as gangs at midnight.

I could look straight ahead and tremble
with my own adrenaline, the way stars hiss

and twinkle, dying, being born.
You could philosophize West on Foster

on the intrinsic meditation of snowfall.
We could meet at the Shell on California,

just like that bump hilariously into flame,
our bodies a perfect impulse of grace.

Torque

The day the funnels jockey like speeding UFOs along Bernard,
break from the blackened West like arms of a raging amoeba
to crash a path along Chicago's North Branch,
East on Foster, scissoring oaks, severing limbs
with the abandon and logic of a bowling team of gods, you
quit Choi's True Value and I gaze with longing
at photos of Wyoming, Tetons a cathedral of tranquility. It's
easy to die with your heart pounding in the sun parlor
surrounded by stained glass and flying buttresses.
Easy. When I run in circles from window to door,
back and forth with ontological questions tapping my skull
like *Which wall is a load-bearing wall?* or
Was this a warning or a watch? I know myself
puny and hysterical, craven and candescent, a star
imploding in the great order. I wish on myself.
I wish I wish I wish but everything is elemental—Lori
walking up Kimball without a clue, the old dog peeing
one block over, biting at hailstones. The cloud
passing by so quickly, the landlord says: What tornado?
And invites me to drink his booze. I'm obsessed with wind.
Green alien air, molecules torquing in the thunder, that leap
at the roof of the house like a crazed bionic, neither
friend nor foe, only bigger than everything that exists—
addiction, ad firms, computers, sex. Lori
turns the corner and the old dog rummages through recycling,
and all the photographs that were on my desk
that are now on the floor lie still as the dead. What's hard
is in the clearing that follows the noise like a thief,
that siphon of sweet adrenalin, all the wild horses, grazing.

Ice

We were driving down the Kennedy having a great time guessing old groups Spinners Commodores La Belle maybe I was driving fast we'd been cold for a month not regular cold scary the kind that wears you down twenty forty below dark so cold you know hell is scratchy wool and miles of hard ice forget heat and everything suddenly stopped the Lincoln which was not our Lincoln but my sister's boyfriend's Lincoln not even his but the leased whim of a fired employee crashed into the back of a steel-gray Mercedes Benz you could feel the ice eat your bones your bumpers the plastic grill curling up the back of the Mercedes Jesus that Lincoln imploded *good old American* the Mercedes owner said as we shook in the ridiculous cold cars whizzing down the frozen highway and Lori's arm shot across my chest like a mother's we'd been spoons sleeping on the sunny couch earlier while the temperature reached a record low in Chicago my ex-husband used to say stop breathing on my back Maureen the only thing I remember about the crash is the way Lori's left arm reached out and saved me from ice crystals on the windshield she said whenever I breathe on her back she melts.

A Flicker of Apocalypse

If the man who called you *nigger* in Dominick's parking lot
had only dialed 1-800-882-Mary earlier today,
he may have been a better Boy Scout. I bet
his wife would be patting him right now, saying: Meat loaf?
It seems there's been heavy-duty Jesus activity
on the East Coast lately and His Mother is behind it.
I see Him bodysurfing in the Atlantic, sharing parables
of large Northshore families and small sea urchins
with teenagers and sandy toddlers. I wonder where
He's hiding—prefab in Wantagh? Coach house in Old Westbury?
We'd been supermarket shopping as usual, a little
decaf, a few oranges, and a skinny man spits the word.
It sounds like *igga* or *neeah,* but you get the point,
and you look at him with one of your kiss-of-death looks,
your obeah-in-the-blood-there's-a-knife-in-my-pocket glower,
and his wife begins to pull on his sleeve like a little girl,
whimpering. And clouds marshal in from the South Side.
And I swear the lights click on at this exact moment.
Every pigeon stands still. Every Toyota. Only the streamers
and banners over Dominick's parking lot rustle in the wind.
I send you my message by archangel—Honey, between us
we could choke this man before the courtesy patrol
arrives to collect his cart. In reality, his wife dragged him away,
and we stood shaking in the light of the all-night supermarket
until the archangel released Chicago and carried us home.

Endometriosis

I was on the train and I was feeling a feeling of well-being and I thought about that, how I was feeling a feeling of well-being. And we pulled into the station at Clark & Division and the doors of the train kept opening letting more people in. We sat there a long time, everyone getting madder, then we puffed to the next station where they said we were disabled and we pushed out of the train like milkweed. So all that really happened today when I felt a feeling of well-being was that a train on the Howard line broke down. On the Congress-O'Hare, a woman jumped in front of a train, same city, same day, same species.

It's the time when old becomes older and everything increases the way water bubbles when you're not watching. Find all the drugs and put them in your shoe, you can find that love here like lovely cells lovely as all the minutes the reasons call me swan. You could call it freer than all the heavens the doors before us like assemblies the name of all swans is swan. You can hear the song you can watch the water slide down the glass and into the shoe. Let's keep it going, never mind the fact that it's over, never mind the silence that comes between musics. You're here, I'm here, there's nothing in between but nothing. You can fill it, and after you fill it, let it empty.

Kind Heart, Cushy Endometriosis.

Remember how scary the word *desert*? How everyone died there when we were kids, crawling on their bellies to the nearest mirage? Come to find out deserts are not a good sign for the Earth. They're dead places becoming deader, like when I was at the door of Death Valley in high summer and someone said: "You go in there and you'll never come out, rookie, Yankee, little naive girl."

Now you're in a cab traveling north on Michigan. You're not in Michigan but you're close getting closer all your cells leaning toward the Upper Peninsula over the Mackinac bridge. Every time the cab sounds its horn you swell as if you're an eardrum or the lake is entering your dead body. A great lake stretches on your East side, out there where a child's voice carries at least ten miles. And Michigan is above you waiting like Canada but not as cold and your hair is blistering white like the tops of pines at Pictured Rocks. The taxi travels so fast your face is plastered back in the wind, nothing is in your way now—not the future in your uterus or the hidden cells making their way like ice around your ovaries. You've got the Devil in your blue-dress eyes shooting flames at oncoming traffic. He drives away like an old tornado. *Welcome to Chicago,* says the back of His T-shirt. You're caught between Him and the deep blue lake.

—•—•—•—

Nostradamus Predicts the Destruction of Chicago

Radiation bubbles beneath the skin.
I'm sick with indeterminacy, the way
light seeps in, thickens the blood with neon.

Strontium in my breast milk, that onion-
skin glint on the freshest salami.
Radiation bubbles beneath the skin

of five-legged calves, poor sucking orphans
of cold war. What did Nostradamus say,
scary sights filled to the brim with neon,

about the balding spot of the man
upstairs, a whirling insomniac? *Hey,*
radiation bubbles beneath the skin

in Batavia, top quarks and a boson
so wraithlike and belligerent they claim
a small bang might sicken the Earth with neon.

When the God Particle collides with its twin,
the Anti-God, I'd rather leap away
where bubbles flit, bereft of radiation,
and light, neon god of gases, thickens.

Suite for Violence

(Garrison-on-Hudson)

The West is over there, the prairie with its needle grasses, the cottonwoods aching with sex in June. The river laps around me like stereo, like footsteps. The lights go up in Rockland. I fear no sound. There is no tide and the river laps the stones. There is absolutely nothing left of us in the wind in the water. I can count on the river, the rattlers, the fading light, the tide diminished and golden and this rushed ending, this coming before I am found in all this calm by the river, the valley inside me. I am soon to grow as large as Hudson, this old life rushing toward the Atlantic from a rip in the clouds.

(What She Did)

I took it like high tide, I was cave and you poured into me. The sea in your fingers inside me. The sea in your mouth that opened and drank me like the juices of apricots and figs. It's my worth, this receptivity—how I'm praised as you pour your electricity, lava, hot wax, as I catch your phlegm, the collection of your angry tales. I'm porcelain, and you lavish me with your fevered secretions.

(Counseling the Witness)

Whatever you do don't talk. It's hard enough you can't get going with the parameters of love beating on your head like a father's voice. Nothing can stop this fabrication. If I were about to murder my lover I would be nuts too. Does it help to remember which she might be—murderer, murderess? I'm watching her come toward me like a murderer. She is not holding the box cutter, her words are holding the box cutter—this is how she sounds—sharp gin. You can follow her into oblivion. Still, I will not call 911 because they say *he* and there is no *he* only a woman with long soft breasts and me.

(Erie—the Flight)

Oh my God you might say and you'd be right for all around is the mask of the divine folding us wanting us. You might say something else matters and you'd be right again. Try imagining how big the body becomes when the angel passes over the blood fields. Incorporate love into your speech, skulls on a fence. Nothing as powerless as God, oh God. I fear someone who says my name again and again until the coat vanishes from the seed, until the seed bursts its tiny shelter and crawls forth.

(North Side)

I heard the buzzer during *Roseanne*'s premier show and there you were sweaty and odd your life was in your face and you were gone the good gone I thought: I might die. The *pro bono* said tell me your story and pieces flew back inside me from all around the city. They flew back in and hunkered down to see what I would say. I pointed to the bruises like old cancers, I pointed to my heart, you could hear it whir inside my chest for recognition. I pointed to the spaces between my nerve endings where something soothed and cajoled. All my pieces waited on my shoulders for the benediction. I stuttered their names. I blessed them.

—•—•—•—

Near Wild Heaven

She said: The difference between us is I dance on my heels, you dance on your toes. She said: You move your head up and down, I move mine from side to side. My shoulders go like this (makes figure eights with shoulders), yours go like this (a see-saw). My feet go *Thriller,* yours go *Material Girl.* Then she took off from the middle of the room like the Only One, the prima terpsichorean Senufo American, *lotsa body & cultural heritage,* I couldn't help it, I loved her because she was a whirling fire leading me straight to the burning heart of God. I was caught in her exhaust fan sucking me out to the roofs of Harlem like a Lois Lane and I cried from the forty nights on Earth while she licked the salt right off my face, the skin from my bleach-white bones. I said: The difference between us is a sliver of sun, I turn this way (45° angle away from the sun in one direction), you turn that way (45° angle away from the sun in the other direction). I hold the prism like this (one hand), you hold it like this (with two), people shading their eyes from something sudden and inexplicable. And she couldn't help it, she left the ground on my consonants and vowels, she loved to swim in my jet stream, take off in my eager air, head wind, tail wind, cooling offshore breeze. We were near wild heaven. We were Garland and Hendrix, we sang with old tongues, we burned bright before we fell, like wishes, into the unconditional sea.

—•—•—•—

Whining Prairie

I don't want to die in this wild onion smelly belly mire of the Midwest stinking marsh this drenchy swaley swamp but I might and who would note the fragrant corruption of my poor *élan* this moorish bog this poachy fen who come from sea with salt and myrrh to burn my rotting flesh? I don't want to fail in grass that stabs my neck this turkey foot as tall as life no roses for my ghostly face my face facedown in chicory and culver's root get these nettles off of me that milkweed from my mouth your thistles catnip purple phlox your funeral mint you've never seen a mermaid in your livelong buckwheat life? I'd rather not allow it lie on land that's locked near fetid ponds this glacial runoff promised conch and bass I'm innocent at poolside foreign standing stagnant pocket plash and lakey sump you'll find me in your placid blue I'll gnaw a hole my teeth as long as lurid lurking coasts. Don't want to twist to Oz in funnel rage of shopping mall and trailer park your horizontal lightning hailstone shelters dug beneath the earth your warnings and your watches trees uptorn your vessels lost in scolding felon wind. I'd sooner die in outer space unlucky astrogirl baloonish letting go to float and float in cyberspace or innerspace. On Mars in bars or cars at camp of cramps in June beneath the King of Beers the Eagle on the Jersey Pike beside the boy who pinched me hard and kissed me young as I was I'd rather die where the ocean drowned me thirteen times then spit me back to life.

The Freezing Point of the Universe

I used to speak in anagrams during sex no wonder
you often left me for girls uninterested in the shift

between "Fawlty Towers" and *flowery twats*. Scold me.
Whenever I think in four-dimensional hypercubic

numerals (1, 16, 81, 256, and so on) you have the right
to demand a simple lunch (pot roast, corn) and tip

me on my head for equilibrium. You're off again I know it,
eyes glazed with dull numbers (although the set

of dull numbers is a null set, go figure). Randomness
steeps in the eye of the beholder; willfulness percolates.

Asked to choose a random number between 10 and 20
you confidently choose 17 like everyone else, a maximally

unremarkable number and here is the catch:
You wish I were one of the Nine Virtuous Women don't you,

the middle pretty sister of the Seven Sisters of Sorrow
and who can blame you. All this talk of radios and "10-codes."

In Shippensburg, Pennsylvania, a 10-45 means "automobile
collision." Elsewhere in the same commonwealth

it stands for "carcass of an unlucky beast." In Maine,
"domestic disturbance." 10-4, Good Buddy. The difference

between the number of pebbles in Newton's calculus
and this four-room house which exhausts the potential

for expansion in the dimensions of width and depth
seems a churlish substitute for the flinty accolades you've been

dealing me lately. And why shouldn't you. Absolute Zero
is where it all begins, the clean slate. Walk out now, you're freezing.

Miss Molly Rockin' in the House of Blue Light

Now you trade your wings for incarnation, commit a quick sin and leap into technicolor, you're visible as sweat, your feet leave prints. Is the desert dead as they say? The hummingbird sharpens her beak then disappears, unsolved caper, arrow of possibility. There is no best time to move, I think, only that moment when you can, when the plate tilts and the peas fall off, when the window opens and the wind sucks you through. Here's the posture of free will, the wind pulling you with your feet firm on either side. I'm gone in a day, sleeping bag, arrow pointing *Go,* that sly permissive. I set off in a white Mazda, low to the ground with sleek lines screaming "Ticket me!" Eighty miles per hour, ninety. In St. Louis, I switch to something indigo with the lines of a shadow and slip South and West. Yukka, rabbits, bubonic plague. I need the same heat on me as in me, dry and crisp, to be the only water for miles around. Bugs hover like disciples, bright revelation on exposed flesh. The humans are pruney and caught in a grin. Everything looms at night as if listening to see if I'll break, if my prayer will lift me to the tops of rocks then throw me to the canyon floor crying *Whoa.* Ghosts walk the canyon talking about nothing much. The one who drew me in a game of straws approaches my tent, leans on my bladder and attaches electrodes to my heart. Still, I pee on red earth, hear death stroll away, silent as ants on an inchworm. When the rain comes I dream of sex, the kind you wake up to, glowing.

Acknowledgments

Grateful acknowledgment is made to the following publications in which the poems first appeared:

The Atlantic Monthly: "The Zen of Crime"

B-City: "Priest"

Boston Review: "Miss Molly Rockin' in the House of Blue Light"

Columbia: A Magazine of Poetry and Prose: "When I Wore a Garter Belt"

Fish Stories: "Ice"

Green Mountains Review: "Fiddleheads," "Found Liturgy," "Jesus & Puberty," "When I Was Straight"

Greensboro Review: "When I Was a Secretary"

Icarus: "When I Was a Junkie"

Indiana Review: "Astronomy," "Torque"

Lit.: "Betty"

New Letters: "Near Wild Heaven"

The New Republic: "Lateral Time" (as "Body Parts")

Paris Review: "A Flicker of Apocalypse," "Vows of Chastity and Indulgence," "Woman Circling Lake"

Ploughshares: "When I Was White"

Poetry: "Romancing Debussy"

Prairie Schooner: "The Church of Scrabble"

Quarter After Eight: "Little Ice Age," "Pluperfect," "Endometriosis" (as "The Ronzoni Madonna"), "The Seven Undefined Mathematical Expressions," "Whining Prairie"

Rhino: "Nostradamus Predicts the Destruction of Chicago"

Witness: "Nostradamus Predicts the Destruction of New York"

—•—•—•—

"Near Wild Heaven," "Jesus & Puberty," "Lateral Time" (as "Body Parts"), "Little Ice Age," "Ice," "Endometriosis" (as "The Ronzoni Madonna"), "Whining Prairie," and "Miss Molly Rockin' in the House of Blue Light," were included (some in different form) in the chapbook *Miss Molly Rockin',* published by Thorngate Road, 1998, Jim Elledge, series ed.

"When I Was Straight" was reprinted in *Not for the Academy: Lesbian Poets*, Lilian Mohin, ed. (London).

“Fiddleheads” was reprinted in *The Best American Poetry 1997,* James Tate and David Lehman, eds.

“The Zen of Crime” was reprinted in *The Prague Review.*

“Ice” was also printed (in slightly different form and with Lori Anderson) in *Portraits of Love: Lesbians Writing About Love,* Susan Fox Rogers & Linda Smukler, eds.

“Suite for Violence” was printed in *The Wild Good,* B. Gates, ed.

—•—•—•—

“The Church of Scrabble” is after Julie Caffey’s performance piece, “Sacred Geometry.” It’s for Julie.

“Found Liturgy” begins with two lines by Charles Simic, from *The World Doesn’t End;* Olive Oyl quote was by her originator, E.C. Segar.

“A Flicker of Apocalypse” takes its title from Amy Clampitt’s poem, “‘Eighty-Nine.” It’s for Lori.

In “Near Wild Heaven,” *lotsa body & cultural heritage* is from the poem “lotsa body & cultural heritage/” by Ntozake Shange in her collection, *nappy edges.* The title is also a song by R.E.M.

“Miss Molly Rockin’ in the House of Blue Light” is from “Good Golly, Miss Molly,” music and lyrics by Robert A. Blackwell and John Marascalco. It’s for Sarah in New Mexico.

—•—•—•—

The author wishes to express her sincere gratitude to the National Endowment for the Arts, the Illinois Arts Council, the Ludwig Vogelstein Foundation, and the Ragdale Foundation for providing funds and time for much of this work.

To Marilyn Hacker, Emily Bowe, Jennifer Bowe, Deborah Digges, Roger Weingarten; and to Cin, Linda B., Lori, Nick, Sarah, Zoe, and H.P.: love and thanks for the faith.

Also by Maureen Seaton

The Sea among the Cupboards
Fear of Subways
Furious Cooking
Exquisite Politics (with Denis Duhamel)

Chapbooks

Miss Molly Rockin'
Oyl (with Denise Duhamel)

Other Books in the

CONTEMPORARY CLASSICS POETRY SERIES

Animal Soul, by Bob Hicok
The Glowing River, by Jack Myers
Roman Fever, by Marcus Cafagña